What's Living at Your Place?

Bruce Chapman

Learning Media

Contents

Introduction

Maybe you don't know it, but you could have house guests. If your home is warm and dry, you might have all kinds of insects and other small creatures living there with you.

A housefly landing on a piece of cake

Most of the time you don't even know your little visitors are there. Some are too small to be seen without a magnifying glass. Some will only come out at night. Others hide under the furniture or crawl into cracks in the wall or floor. A few may even live in your bed!

Sometimes, these small animals can be pests. They may bite you, eat the food in your pantry, chew the carpets, or just annoy you. That's when it's time to take some action!

Bug Zoo

There are bugs in the pantry.
There are bugs in the wall.
There are bugs in the living room
and running down the hall.

There are bugs on your potted plants.
There are bugs in your bed.
There are bugs on your favorite chair
and nibbling on your head.

Have you wondered where they came from?
Do you know what they do?
Are you puzzled why they live there
and why your home is like a zoo?

1. Night Raiders

In many countries, cockroaches are a common insect found in people's houses. Cockroaches first lived on Earth before dinosaurs did, over 300,000,000 years ago.

Why have cockroaches been around for so long? Well, their bodies are flat and slippery, so they can squeeze into cracks that most other creatures can't get into. And, if you've ever had cockroaches at your place, you'll know they are fast runners and are very difficult to catch.

The Cockroach

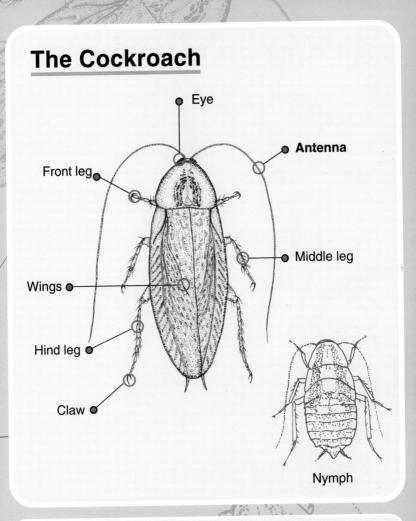

Eye

Antenna

Front leg

Middle leg

Wings

Hind leg

Claw

Nymph

The cockroach's body is brown or black. Adult cockroaches have wings, but they don't often fly. Young cockroaches are called "nymphs."

Life Cycle of the Cockroach

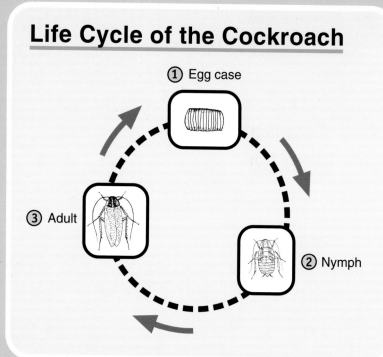

① Egg case

③ Adult

② Nymph

The female cockroach lays her eggs in a dark brown **egg case** that looks like a small purse. She carries this egg case on the end of her body for about a month and then leaves it in a warm, damp place. After about a day, the young nymphs hatch. It can take a year or more before the nymphs become adults.

Habitat and Habits

Cockroaches like places that are dark and warm. The kitchen and bathroom are favorite places. If you disturb a cockroach, it will scurry away from the light and slip into the nearest crack.

Cockroaches are **scavengers**. They usually come out at night to look for food. They will eat almost anything, including humans' food, garbage, and dead plants and animals. They even live in sewers and can come into your home through the drainpipes. In this way, they can spread germs, so they're not welcome guests.

Pest Control

When cockroaches become a problem in your house, you can:

- clear away food scraps and store food in airtight containers
- plug up cracks where cockroaches might live
- use special cockroach traps
- spray with insecticide if things get really bad.

2. Itchy Biters

Do you sometimes get itchy bites? These may be caused by mosquitoes or fleas – two very small insects that often come into our homes.

Adult flea on cat fur

Adult mosquito

The Mosquito

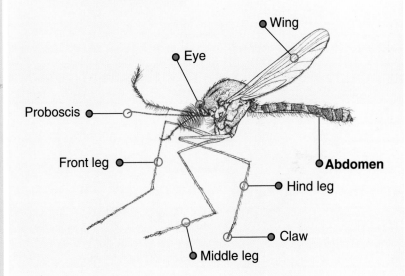

Mosquitoes are small, two-winged flies. They are very common in **tropical** countries. Female mosquitoes need to feed on blood to produce eggs. They jab your skin with their sharp **proboscis** to suck up some blood. It's the **saliva** in their bite that makes your skin itchy.

Life Cycle of the Mosquito

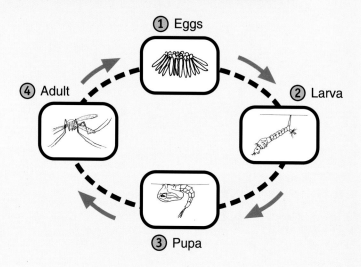

① Eggs

④ Adult

② Larva

③ Pupa

Mosquitoes lay their eggs on the surface of still water. The eggs hatch into **larvae**, which are called wrigglers. After a while, the wrigglers turn into **pupae**, which grow into adults. One life cycle takes about two weeks.

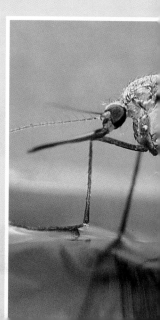

Mosquitoes can be serious pests in tropical countries because they spread human diseases like **malaria** and **yellow fever**.

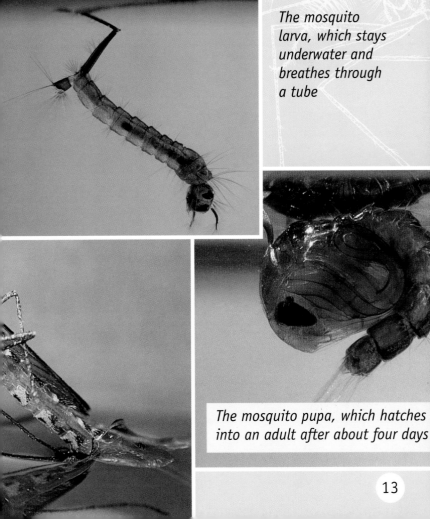

The mosquito larva, which stays underwater and breathes through a tube

The mosquito pupa, which hatches into an adult after about four days

The Flea

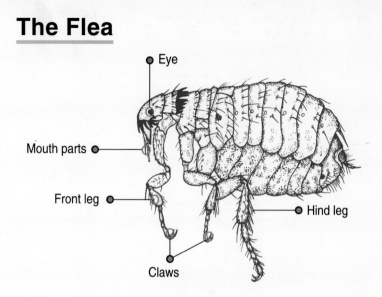

Eye

Mouth parts

Front leg

Hind leg

Claws

Fleas are small, brown insects. The sides of a flea's body are flat. This allows it to move quickly through hair and fur. Fleas don't have wings, but the adults are amazing jumpers. They can leap as much as 12 inches. To equal such a leap, a person would have to jump over 200 yards in one go!

An adult flea

Life Cycle of the Flea

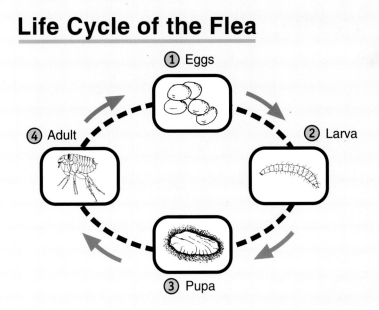

① Eggs

② Larva

③ Pupa

④ Adult

Female fleas lay their eggs on your cat or dog or in the places where your pet sleeps. When the eggs hatch, the young larvae look like tiny, white worms. After about two weeks, the worm makes a pupa. Inside the pupa, the worm grows into an adult flea. The adult flea then hops onto the nearest warm-blooded animal – maybe your pet or maybe you!

Habitat and Habits

Most kinds of fleas live on rats, mice, and other animals that live in nests, such as rabbits and birds. The thick fur or hair on your cat or dog is also the perfect home for a flea. Adult fleas bite skin in order to feed on blood, and this can make your pet scratch like crazy. But sometimes you don't know that there are fleas living at your house until they start to bite you.

Pest Control

If you find that fleas are using your cat or dog as a walking hotel, you can:
- use a flea collar
- use special drops or powder
- clean your pet's bed and blanket
- bathe and brush your pet regularly.

Because fleas feed on blood, they can spread disease from animal to animal – and to humans. It was fleas living on rats that spread the **bubonic plague**.

3. Scary Spiders

Many people don't like spiders because they think they look scary or because they are afraid of being bitten. In fact, most spiders won't bite you unless you pick them up or they get caught in your clothing. House spiders, jumping spiders, and wolf spiders often come inside. Others, such as the trapdoor spider, are usually found outside.

The house spider, which can be found inside at any time of the year

The Spider

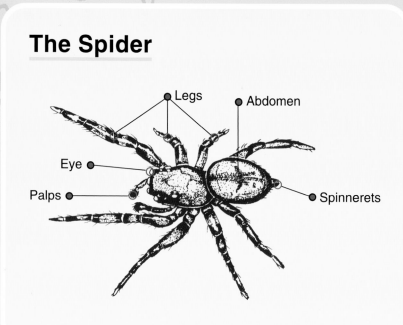

Spiders are not insects. Insects have three parts to their body – a head, **thorax**, and abdomen. Spiders only have two parts. And insects have six legs, but spiders have eight. Spiders also never have wings like some insects do.

Life Cycle of the Spider

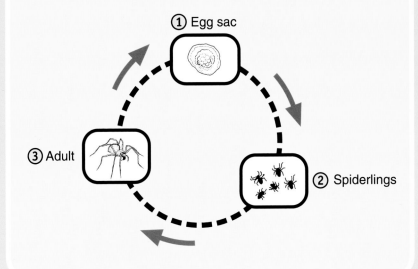

① Egg sac

② Spiderlings

③ Adult

Female spiders lay eggs in an **egg sac**. The eggs hatch inside the sac, and young spiderlings come out soon after. The spiderlings **molt** several times before they become adults. The life cycle of most spiders takes less than 12 months.

Habitat and Habits

Spiders like a quiet life. They often hide in the basement or in dark cupboards. Most spiders make silk for their webs or nests. They use silk to make their egg sacs too.

Spiders are **predators**. They come out at night to feed. Some, like the wolf spider, are hunters and track down their **prey**. Others, like the trapdoor spider, sit and wait for their prey to come by and then pounce. Usually, the spiders you might see in your house are the ones that spin webs to catch prey.

Spiders need water. That's why you might find one in the bath or shower, looking for a drop of water to drink.

The jumping spider, which has the best eyesight of any spider. You often find jumping spiders on house plants.

Pest Control

Spiders are helpful visitors. They catch and eat other insect pests, such as flies and mosquitoes. If you find spiders in your house:

- leave them alone if you can
- scoop them up in a jar and put them outside if you need to
- spray with a regular fly spray if they become a problem.

4. Buzzy Beasts

The most buzzy insects are flies. The buzzing of a fly is the sound of its wings beating. A housefly can beat its wings about 200 times a second. That's fast but not as fast as the mosquito. A mosquito can beat its wings an amazing 600 times a second.

In warm weather, lots of different flies come into our homes. Houseflies and blow flies are the most common kinds. Blow flies have a very good sense of smell. They will fly a long way toward the smell of food cooking or the smell of rotting meat. Houseflies don't usually fly very far.

The Fly

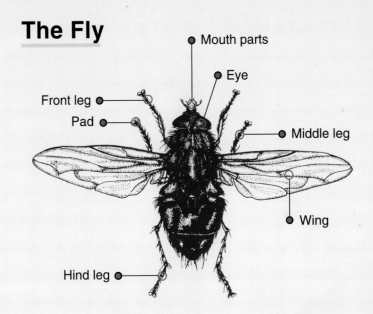

Mouth parts

Eye

Front leg

Pad

Middle leg

Wing

Hind leg

Houseflies have only one pair of wings. Their bodies are covered with fine hairs. Flies can walk upside down on the ceiling or on slippery windows and mirrors. They can do this because they have sticky pads on their feet.

Life Cycle of the Fly

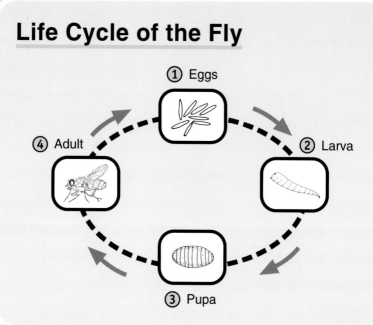

① Eggs

② Larva

③ Pupa

④ Adult

Houseflies usually lay their eggs in rotting things, such as dead plants or meat. It only takes the eggs about a day to hatch into larvae called **maggots**. The maggots feed on the rotting plant or meat. When a maggot is fully grown, it turns into a pupa. Then, after about five days, an adult fly hatches. In summer, an adult housefly lives for about three weeks. That doesn't seem long, but during that time the female can lay hundreds of eggs.

Habitat and Habits

Because flies crawl over everything, they pick up germs. When a fly walks on food, it leaves germs behind. Then, if you eat the food, the germs get into your stomach. Sometimes these germs can make you sick.

Flies like warm weather. When it gets colder, they slow down.

Pest Control

In warm weather, when flies start buzzing about, people stop them coming into the houses by:

- getting rid of garbage and food scraps
- making sure that food is kept in sealed containers
- putting fly screens on doors and windows
- using sticky flytraps
- zapping them with fly spray.

5. A Mouse in the House

It's not only insects and spiders that like living at your place – mice do too. Mice like living with us because houses are warm places and there is usually food to eat.

House mice are busy animals. They scamper about day and night looking for food. Their eyesight is not very good, but they can hear noises, and they have a very good sense of smell.

Some children keep mice as pets. Pet mice are kept in cages.

The Mouse

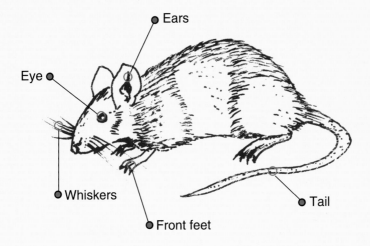

Ears

Eye

Whiskers

Front feet

Tail

The house mouse has soft gray or brown fur and a pinkish tail. It has a long, narrow nose with whiskers on each side. A house mouse will eat almost anything that people eat. It can cause a lot of damage with its sharp front teeth. In the pantry, it can chew through paper and plastic containers to get to food.

Life Cycle of the Mouse

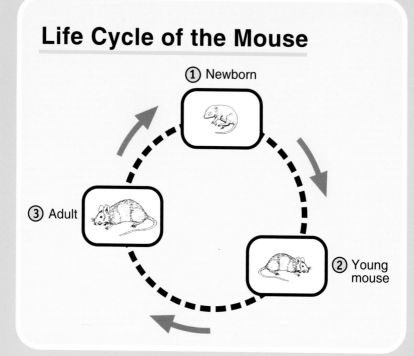

① Newborn

③ Adult

② Young mouse

A female house mouse can have babies about every month. Newborn mice have pink skin and no fur, and their eyes are closed. By the time they are two weeks old, they are covered in fur and they can open their eyes.

It takes about six weeks for baby mice to grow to be adults. Then they are ready to have baby mice themselves.

Habitat and Habits

House mice build nests in warm, quiet places. They line their nests with all kinds of things like feathers, fur, and material. House mice do not move far from their nests. When they do go out and about, they try not to be seen. They move around the edges of a room and under furniture.

Pet cats and dogs are the worst enemies of house mice.

Pest Control

People don't like sharing their homes with mice – unless they're pet mice in a cage. Mice can move very fast and can squeeze through the smallest of cracks. So, to stop mice coming into your house:

- block up all the cracks where they might find their way in
- don't leave food out on counters overnight.

If mice become a problem, people usually put out poison bait or traps. Cats (and some dogs) are very good at getting rid of mice, too.

The House Guests in This Book

These are just some of the animals and insects that might be living at your place. We haven't even had time to look at silverfish, pill bugs, book lice, bats, snakes, birds ... the list goes on and on. Maybe you could do some research on one of these "house guests" yourself.

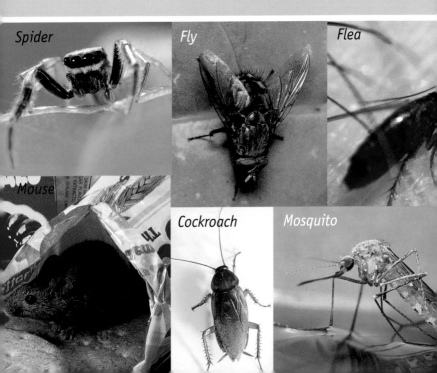

Spider

Fly

Flea

Mouse

Cockroach

Mosquito

Glossary

(These words are printed in bold type
the first time they appear in the book.)

abdomen: the back section of an insect or spider

antenna: a feeler on the head of an insect

bubonic plague: a disease spread by fleas living on rats

egg case: a hard pouch that keeps eggs safe

egg sac: a silk cover that protects a spider's eggs

larva(e): the stage after the egg in an insect life cycle

maggots: another name for the larvae of flies

malaria: a disease that can be carried by mosquitoes

molt: to shed skin

predators: an animal or insect that attacks and feeds
on other animals or insects

prey: an animal or insect that is hunted by other animals
or insects for food

proboscis: mouthparts found on some insects

pupa(e): an insect in the stage between larva and adult
in their life cycle

saliva: a liquid made by mouthparts

scavengers: animals or insects that eat anything
they find

thorax: the middle section of an insect

tropical: near the equator; hot and humid

yellow fever: a disease often carried by mosquitoes

Index